D1880698

PSYCHOLOGY
OF THE
STOCK MARKET

PSYCHOLOGY
OF THE
STOCK MARKET

By

G. C. SELDEN

GYAN

Published by

Gyan Publishing House
5, Ansari Road
Daryaganj, New Delhi-110002
Phone: 011-47034999, 9811692060
E-mail: books@gyanbooks.com

Distribution Network
gyanbooks.com
India, USA, Canada, UK, Australia, France

© Publisher

All rights reserved. No part of this work may be reproduced, stored, adapted, or transmitted in any form or by any means, electronic, mechanical, photocopying, micro-filming, recording or otherwise, or translated in any language, without the prior written permission of the copyright owner and the publisher.

ISBN : 978-81-212-9794-3 (PB)
First Published, 1912

2nd Impression 2023

Printed at: Gyan Press, Delhi.

The book is sold subject to the condition that it shall not, by way of trade or otherwise, be lent, resold, hired out, or otherwise circulated without the prior publisher's written consent.

PSYCHOLOGY OF THE STOCK MARKET
Author: G. C. SELDEN

PSYCHOLOGY

OF THE

STOCK MARKET

By G. C. Selden

Author of "Trade Cycles," "What Makes the Market ?"
Etc.

PREFACE

THIS book is based upon the belief that the movements of prices on the exchanges are dependent to a very large degree on the mental attitude of the investing and trading public. It is the result of years of study and experience as fellow at Columbia University, news writer, statistician, on the editorial staff of THE MAGAZINE OF WALL STREET, etc.

The book is intended chiefly as a practical help to that considerable part of the community which is interested, directly or indirectly, in the markets; but it is hoped that it may also have some scientific value as a preliminary discussion in a new field, where opportunities for further research seem almost unlimited.

G. C. SELDEN.

New York, May 28, 1912.

CONTENTS.

I—The Speculative Cycle

MOST experienced professional traders in the stock market will readily admit that the minor fluctuations, amounting to perhaps five or ten dollars a share in the active speculative issues, are chiefly psychological. They result from varying attitudes of the public mind, or, more strictly, from the mental attitudes of those persons who are interested in the market at the time.

Such fluctuations may be, and often are, based on "fundamental" conditions—that is, on real changes in the dividend prospects of the stocks affected or on variations in the earning power of the corporations represented —and again they may not. The broad movements of the market, covering periods of months or even years, are always the result of general financial conditions; but the smaller intermediate fluctuations represent changes in the state of the public mind, which may or may not coincide with alterations in basic factors.

To bring out clearly the degree to which psychology enters into the stock market problem from day to day, it is only necessary to reproduce a conversation between professional traders such as may be heard almost any day in New street or in the neighboring cafés.

"Well, what do you know?" says one trader to the other.

"Just covered my Steel," is the reply. "Too much company. Everybody seems to be short."

"Everybody I've seen thinks just as you do. Each one has covered because he thinks everybody else is short—still the market doesn't rally much. I don't believe there's much short interest left, and if that's the case we shall get another break."

"Yes, that's what they all say—and

they've all sold short again because they think everybody else has covered. I believe there's just as much short interest now as there was before."

It is evident that this series of inversions might be continued indefinitely. These alert mental acrobats are doing a succession of flip-flops, each one of which leads up logically to the next, without ever arriving at a final stopping-place.

The main point of their argument is that the state of mind of a man short of the market is radically different from the state of mind of one who is long. Their whole study, in such a conversation, is the mental attitude of those interested in the market. If a majority of the volatile class of in-and-out traders are long, many of them will hasten to sell on any sign of weakness and a decline will result. If the majority are short, they will buy on any development of strength and an advance may be expected.

The psychological aspects of speculation may be considered from two points of view, equally important. One question is, What effect do varying mental attitudes of the public have upon the course of prices? How is the character of the market influenced by psychological conditions?

A second consideration is, How does the mental attitude of the individual trader affect his chances of success? To what extent, and how, can he overcome the obstacles placed in his pathway by his own hopes and fears, his timidities and his obstinacies?

These two points of view are so closely involved and intermingled that it is almost impossible to consider either one alone. It will be necessary to take up first the subject of speculative psychology as a whole, and later to attempt to draw conclusions both as to its effects upon the market and its influence upon the fortunes of the individual trader.

As a convenient starting point it may be well to trace briefly the history of the typical speculative cycle, which runs its course over and over, year after year, with infinite slight variations but with substantial similarity, on every stock exchange and in every speculative market of the world—and presumably will continue to do so as long as prices are fixed by the competition of buyers and sellers, and as long as human beings seek a profit and fear a loss.*

Beginning with a condition of dullness and inactivity, with small fluctuations and very slight public interest, prices begin to rise, at first almost imperceptibly. No special reason appears for the advance, and it is generally thought to be merely temporary, due to small professional operations. There is, of course, some short interest in the market, mostly, at this time, of the character sometimes called a "sleeping"

*The writer discussed this subject rather fully in the *Quarterly Journal of Economics,* Vol. XVI, No. 2. The article will also be found extensively summarized and quoted in Vol. VII of "Modern Business," edited by Joseph French Johnson, Dean of New York University School of Commerce.

short interest. An active speculative stock is never entirely free from shorts.

As there is so little public speculation at this period in the cycle, there are but few who are willing to sell out on so small an advance, hence prices are not met by any large volume of profit-taking. The smaller professionals take the short side for a turn, with the idea that trifling fluctuations are the best that can be hoped for at the moment and must be taken advantage of if any profits are to be secured. This class of selling brings prices back almost to their former dead level.

Soon another unostentatious upward movement begins, carrying prices a trifle higher than the first. A few shrewd traders take the long side, but the public is still unmoved and the sleeping short interest—most of it originally put out at much higher figures—still refuses to waken.

Gradually prices harden further and finally advance somewhat sharply. A few of the more timid shorts cover, perhaps to save a part of their profits or to prevent their trades from running into a loss. The fact that a bull turn is coming now penetrates through another layer of intellectual density and another wave of traders take the long side. The public notes the advance and begins to think some further upturn is possible, but that there will be plenty of opportunities to buy on substantial reactions.

Strangely enough, these reactions, except of the most trifling character, do not appear. Waiting buyers do not get a satisfactory chance to take hold. Prices begin to move up faster. There is a halt from time to time, but when a real reaction finally comes the market looks "too weak to buy," and when it starts up again it often does so with a sudden leap that leaves would-be purchasers far in the rear.

At length the more stubborn bears become alarmed and begin to cover in large volume. The market "boils," and to the short who is watching the tape, seems likely to shoot through the ceiling at almost any moment. However firm may be his bearish convictions, his nervous system eventually gives out under this continual pounding, and he covers everything "at the market" with a sigh of relief that his losses are no greater.

About this time the outside public begins to reach the conclusion that the market is "too strong to react much," and that the only thing to do is to "buy 'em anywhere." From this source comes another wave of buying, which soon carries prices to new high levels, and purchasers congratulate themselves on their quick and easy profits.

For every buyer there must be a seller—or, more accurately, for every one hundred shares bought one hundred shares must be sold, as the actual number of *persons* buying at this stage is likely to be much greater than the number of *persons* selling. Early in the advance the supply of stocks is small and comes from scattered sources, but as prices rise, more and more holders become satisfied with their profits and willing to sell. The bears, also, begin to fight the advance by by selling short on every quick rise. A stubborn professional bear will often be forced to cover again and again, with a small loss each time, before he finally locates the top and secures a liberal profit on the ensuing decline.

Those selling at this stage are not, as a rule, the largest holders. The largest holders are usually those whose judgment is sound enough, or whose connections are good enough, so that they have made a good deal of money; and neither a sound judgment nor the best advisers are likely to favor selling so early in the advance, when much larger profits can be secured by simply holding on.

The height to which prices can now be carried depends on the underlying conditions. If money is easy and general business prosperous a prolonged bull movement may result, while strained banking resources or depressed trade will set a definite limit to the possible advance. If conditions are bearish, the driving of the biggest shorts to cover will practically end the rise; but in a genuine bull market the advance will continue until checked by sales of stocks held for investment, which come upon the market only when prices are believed to be unduly high.

In a sense, the market is always a contest between investors and speculators. The real investor, looking chiefly to interest return, but by no means unwilling to make a profit by buying low and selling high, is ready, perhaps, to buy his favorite stock at a price which will yield him six per cent. on his investment, or to sell at a price yielding only four per cent. The speculator cares nothing about interest return. He wants to buy before prices go up and to sell short before they go down. He would as soon buy at the top of a big rise at any other time, provided prices are going still higher.

As the market advances, therefore, one investor after another sees his limit reached and his stock sold. Thus the volume of stocks to be carried or tossed from hand to hand by bullish speculators is constantly rolling up like a snowball. On the ordinary intermediate fluctuations, covering five to twenty dollars a share, these sales by investors are small compared with the speculative business. In one hundred shares of a stock selling at 150, the investor has $15,000; but with this sum the speculator can easily carry ten times that number of shares.

The reason why sales by investors are so effective is not because of the actual amount of stock thrown on the market, but because this stock is a permanent load, which will not be got rid of again until prices have suffered a severe decline. What the speculator sells he or some other trader may buy back tomorrow.

The time comes when everybody seems to be buying. Prices become confused. One stock leaps upward in a way to strike terror to the heart of the last surviving short. Another appears almost equally strong, but slips back unobtrusively when nobody is looking, like the frog jumping out of the well in the arithmetic of our boyhood. Still another churns violently in one place, like a side-wheeler stuck on a sand-bar.

Then the market gives a sudden lurch downward, as though in danger of spilling out its unwieldy contents. This is hailed as a "healthy reaction," though it is a mystery whom it can be healthy for, unless it is the shorts. Prices recover again, with everybody happy except a few disgruntled bears, who are rightly regarded with contemptuous amusement.

Curiously, however, there seems to be stock enough for all comers, and the few cranks who have time to bother with such things notice that the general average of prices is now rising very slowly, if at all. The largest speculative holders of stocks, finding a market big enough to absorb their sales, are letting go. And there are always stocks enough to go around. Our big capitalists are seldom entirely out of stocks. They merely have more stocks when prices are low and fewer when prices are high. Moreover, long before there is any danger of the supply running out, plenty of new issues are created.

When there is a general public interest in the stock market, an immense amount of realizing will often be absorbed within three or four days or a week, after which the deluge; but if speculation is narrow, prices may remain around top figures for weeks or months, while big holdings are fed out, a few hundred shares here and a few hundred there, and even then a balance may be left to be thrown over on the ensuing decline at whatever prices can be obtained. Great speculative leaders are far from infallible. They have often sold out too soon and later have seen the market run away to unexpected heights, or have held on too long and have suffered severe losses before they could get out.

In this selling the bull leaders get a good deal of undesired help from the bears. However wary the bulls may be in concealing their sales, their machinations will be discovered by watchful professionals and shrewd chart students, and a considerable sprinkling of short sales will be put out within a few points of the top. This is one of the reasons why the long swings in active speculative stocks are smaller in proportion to price than in inactive specialties of a similar character—contrary to the generally received impression. It is rare that any considerable short interest exists in the inactive stocks.

Once the top-heavy load is overturned, the decline is usually more rapid than the previous advance. The floating supply, now greatly increased, is tossed about from one speculator to another at lower and lower prices. From time to time stocks become temporarily lodged in stubborn hands, so that part of the shorts take fright and cover, causing a sharp upturn; but so long as the load of stocks is still on the market the general course of prices must be downward.

Until investors or big speculative capitalists again come into the market, the load of stocks to be carried by ordinary speculative bulls increases almost continually. There is no lessening of the floating supply of stock certificates in the Street, and there is a gradual increase in the short interest; and of course the bulls have to carry these short sales as well as the actual certificates, since for every seller there must be a buyer, whether the sale be made by a short or a long. Shorts cover again and again on the sharp breaks, but in most cases they put out their lines again, either higher or lower, as opportunity offers. On the average, the short interest is largest at low prices, though there are likely to be periods during the decline when it will be larger than at the final bottom, where buying by shorts often helps to avert panicky conditions.

The length of this decline, like the extent of the preceding advance, depends on fundamental conditions; for both investors and speculative capitalists will come into the market sooner if all conditions are favorable than they will in a stringent money market or when the future prospects of business are unsatisfactory. As a rule, buyers do not appear in force until a "bargain day" appears. This is when, in its downward course, the heavy load of stocks strikes an area honeycombed with stop loss orders. Floor traders seize the opportunity to put out short lines and a general collapse results.

Here are plenty of stocks to be had cheap, and shrewd operators—large and small, but mostly large or on the way to become so—are busy picking them up. The fixed limits of many investors are also reached by the sharp break, and their purchases disappear, to be seen in the Street no more until the next bull turn.

Many shorts cover on such a break, but not all. The sequel to the "bargain day" is a big short interest which has overstayed its market, and a quick rally follows; but when the more urgent shorts get relief, prices sag again and fall into that condition of lethargy from which this consideration of the speculative cycle started.

The movements described are substantially uniform, whether the cycle be one covering a week, a month, or a year. The big cycle includes many intermediate movements, and these movements in turn contain smaller swings. Investors do not participate to any extent in the small swings, but otherwise the forces involved in a three-point turn up and down are substantially the same as those which appear in a thirty-point cycle, though not so easy to identify.

The fact will at once be recognized that the above description is, in essence, a story of human hopes and fears; of a mental attitude, on the part of those interested, resulting from their own position in the market, rather than from any deliberate judgment of conditions: of an unwarranted projection by the public imagination of a perceived present into an unknown though not wholly unknowable future.

Laying aside for the present the influence of fundamental conditions on prices, it is our task to trace out both the causes and the effects of these psychological elements in speculation.

II—Inverted Reasoning and its Consequences

IT is hard for the average man to oppose what appears to be the general drift of public opinion. In the stock market this is perhaps harder than elsewhere; for we all realize that the prices of stocks must, in the long run, be controlled by public opinion. The point we fail to remember is that public opinion in a speculative market is measured in dollars, not in population. One man controlling one million dollars has double the weight of five hundred men with one thousand dollars each. Dollars are the horse-power of the markets—the mere number of men does not signify.

This is why the great body of opinion appears to be bullish at the top and bearish at the bottom. The multitude of small traders must be, as a plain necessity, long when prices are at the top, and short or out of the market at the bottom. The very fact that they *are* long at the top shows that they have been supplied with stocks from some source.

Again, the man with one million dollars is a silent individual. The time when it was necessary for him to talk is past—his money now does the talking. But the one thousand men who have one thousand dollars each are conversational, fluent, verbose to the last degree; and among these smaller traders are the writers—the newspaper and news bureau men, and the manufacturers of gossip for brokerage houses.

It will be observed that the above course of reasoning leads us to the conclusion that most of those who write and talk about the market are more likely to be wrong than right, at least so far as speculative fluctuations are concerned. This is not complimentary to the "moulders of public opinion," but most seasoned newspaper readers will agree that it is true. The press reflects, in a general way, the thoughts of the multitude, and in the stock market the multitude is necessarily, as a logical deduction from the facts of the case, likely to be bullish at high prices and bearish at low.

It has often been remarked that the average man is an optimist regarding his own enterprises and a pessimist regarding those of others. Certainly this is true of the professional trader in stocks. As a result of the reasoning outlined above, he comes habitually to expect that nearly every one else will be wrong, but is, as a rule, confident that his own analysis of the situation will prove correct. He values the opinions of a few persons whom he believes to be generally successful; but aside from these few, the greater the number of the bullish opinions he hears, the more doubtful he becomes about the wisdom of following the bull side.

This apparent contrariness of the market, although easily understood when its causes are analyzed, breeds in professional traders a peculiar sort of skepticism—leads them always to distrust the obvious and to apply a kind of inverted reasoning to almost all stock market problems. Often, in the minds of traders who are not naturally logical, this inverted reasoning assumes the most erratic and grotesque forms, and it accounts for many apparently absurd fluctuations in prices which are commonly charged to manipulation.

For example, a trader starts with this assumption: The market has had a good advance; all the small traders are bullish; somebody must have sold them the stock which they are carrying; hence the big capitalists are probably sold out or short and ready for a reaction or perhaps for a bear market. Then if a strong item of bullish news comes out—one, let us say, that really makes an important change in the situation—he says, "Ah, so this is what they have been bulling the market on! It has been discounted by the previous rise." Or he may say, "They are putting out this bull news to sell stocks on." He proceeds to sell out any long stocks he may have or perhaps to sell short.

His reasoning may be correct or it may not; but at any rate his selling and that of others who reason in a similar way, is likely to produce at least a temporary decline on the announcement of the good news. This decline looks absurd to the outsider and he falls back on the old explanation, "All manipulation."

The same principle is often carried further. You will find professional traders reasoning that favorable figures on the steel industry, for example, have been concocted to enable insiders to sell their Steel; or that gloomy reports are put in circulation to facilitate accumulation. Hence they may act in direct opposition to the news and carry the market with them, for the time at least.

The less the trader knows about the fundamentals of the financial situation the more likely he is to be led astray in conclusions of this character. If he has confidence in the general strength of conditions he may be ready to accept as genuine and natural, a piece of news which he would otherwise receive with cynical skepticism and use as a basis for short sales. If he knows that fundamental conditions are unsound, he will not be so likely to interpret bad news as issued to assist in accumulation of stocks.

The same reasoning is applied to large purchases through brokers known to be associated with capitalists. In fact, in this case we often hear a double inversion, as it were. Such buying may impress the observer in three ways:

1. The "rank outsider" takes it at face value, as bullish.

2. A more experienced trader may say, "If they really wished to get the

stocks they would not buy through their own brokers, but would endeavor to conceal their buying by scattering it among other houses."

3. A still more suspicious professional may turn another mental somersault and say, "They are buying through their own brokers so as to throw us off the scent and make us think someone else is using their brokers as a blind." By this double somersault such a trader arrives at the same conclusion as the outsider.

The reasoning of traders becomes even more complicated when large buying or selling is done openly by a big professional who is known to trade in and out for small profits. If he buys 50,000 shares, other traders are quite willing to sell to him and their opinion of the market is little influenced, simply because they know he may sell 50,000 the next day or even the next hour. For this reason great capitalists sometimes buy or sell through such big professional traders in order to execute their orders easily and without arousing suspicion. Hence the play of subtle intellects around big trading of this kind often becomes very elaborate.

It is to be noticed that this inverted reasoning is useful chiefly at the top or bottom of a movement, when distribution or accumulation is taking place on a large scale. A market which repeatedly refuses to respond to good news after a considerable advance is likely to be "full of stocks." Likewise a market which will not go down on bad news is usually "bare of stocks."

Between the extremes will be found long stretches in which capitalists have very little cause to conceal their position. Having accumulated their lines as low as possible, they are then willing to be known as the leaders of the upward movement and have every reason to be perfectly open in their buying. This condition continues until they are ready to sell. Likewise, having sold as much as they desire, they have no reason to conceal their position further, even though a subsequent decline may run for months or a year.

It is during a long upward movement that the "lamb" makes money, because he accepts facts as facts, while the professional trader is often found fighting the advance and losing heavily because of his over-development of cynicism and suspicion.

The successful trader eventually learns when to invert his natural mental processes and when to leave them in their usual position. Often he develops a sort of instinct which could scarcely be reduced to cold print. But in the hands of the tyro this form of reasoning is exceedingly dangerous, because it permits of putting an alternate construction on any event. Bull news either (1) is significant of a rising trend of prices, or (2) indicates that "they" are trying to make a market to sell on. Bad news may indicate either a genuinely bearish situation or a desire to accumulate stocks at low prices.

The inexperienced operator is therefore left very much at sea. He is playing with the professional's edged tools and is likely to cut himself. Of what use is it for him to try to apply his reason to stock market conditions when every event may be doubly interpreted?

Indeed, it is doubtful if the professional's distrust of the obvious is of much benefit to him in the long run. Most of us have met those deplorable mental wrecks, often found among the "chairwarmers" in brokers' offices, whose thinking machinery seems to have become permanently demoralized as a result of continued acrobatics. They are always seeking an "ulterior motive" in everything. They credit—or debit—Morgan and Rockefeller with the smallest and meanest trickery and ascribe to them the most artful duplicity in matters which those "high financiers" wouldn't stoop to notice. The continual reversal of the mental engine sometimes deranges its mechanism.

Probably no better general rule can

be laid down than the brief one, "Stick to common sense." Maintain a balanced, receptive mind and avoid abstruse deductions. A few further suggestions may, however, be offered:

If you already have a position in the market, do not attempt to bolster up your failing faith by resorting to intellectual subtleties in the interpretation of obvious facts. If you are long or short of the market, you are not an unprejudiced judge, and you will be greatly tempted to put such an interpretation upon current events as will coincide with your preconceived opinion. It is hardly too much to say that this is the greatest obstacle to success. The least you can do is to avoid inverted reasoning in support of your own position.

After a prolonged advance, do not call inverted reasoning to your aid in order to prove that prices are going still higher; likewise after a big break do not let your bearish deductions become too complicated. Be suspicious of bull news at high prices, and of bear news at low prices.

Bear in mind that an item of news usually causes but *one* considerable movement of prices. If the movement takes place before the news comes out, as a result of rumors and expectations, then it is not likely to be repeated after the announcement is made; but if the movement of prices has not preceded, then the news contributes to the general strength or weakness of the situation and a movement of prices may follow.

III—"They"

IF a man entirely unfamiliar with the stock market should spend several days around the Exchange listening to the conversation of all sorts of traders and investors, in order to pick up information about the causes of price movements, the probability is that the most pressing question in his mind at the end of that time would be "Who are 'They?'"

Everywhere he went he would hear about Them. In the customers' rooms of the fractional lot houses he would find young men trading in ten shares and arguing learnedly as to what They were to do next. Tape readers—experts and tyros alike—would tell him that They were accumulating Steel, or distributing Reading. Floor traders and members of the Exchange would whisper that they were told They were going to put the market up, or down, as the case might be. Even sedate investors might inform him that, although the situation was bearish, undoubtedly They would have to put the market temporarily higher in order to unload Their stocks.

This "They" theory of the market is quite as prevalent among successful traders as among beginners—probably more so. There may be room for argument as to why this is so, but as to the fact itself there is no doubt. Whether They are a myth or a definite reality, many persons are making money by studying the market from this point of view.

If you were to go around Wall street and ask various classes of traders who They are, you would get nearly as many different answers as the number of people interviewed. One would say, "The house of Morgan"; another, "Standard Oil and associated interests"—which is pretty broad, when you stop to think of it; another, "The big banking interests";

still another, "Professional traders on the floor"; a fifth, "Pools in the various favorite stocks, which act more or less in concert"; a sixth might say, "Shrewd and successful speculators, whoever and wherever they are"; while to the seventh, They may typify merely active traders as a whole, whom he conceives to make prices by falling over each other to buy or to sell.

Indeed, one writer of no small attainments as a student of market conditions believes that the entire phenomena of the New York stock market are under the control of some one individual, who is presumably, in some way or other, the representative of great associated interests.

It seems obviously impossible to trace to its source, tag and identify any sort of permanent controlling power. The stock markets of the world move pretty much together in the broad cyclical swings, so that such a power would have to consist of a world-wide association of great financial interests, controlling all of the principal security markets. The average observer will find it difficult to masticate and swallow this proposition.

The effort to reduce the science of speculation and investment to an impossible definiteness or an ideal simplicity is, I believe, responsible for many failures. A. S. Hardy, the diplomat, who was formerly a professor of mathematics and wrote books on quaternions, differential calculus, etc., once remarked that the study of mathematics is very poor mental discipline, because it does not cultivate the judgment. Given fixed and certain premises, your mathematician will follow them out to a correct conclusion; but in practical affairs the whole difficulty lies in selecting your premises.

So the market student of a mathematical turn of mind is always seeking a rule or a set of rules—a "sure thing" as traders put it. He would not seek such rules for succeeding in the grocery business or the lumber business; he would, on the contrary, analyze each situation as it arose and act accordingly. The stock market presents itself to my mind as a purely practical proposition. Scientific methods may be applied to any line of business, from stocks to chickens, but this is a very different thing from trying to reduce the fluctuations of the stock market to a basis of mathematical certainty.

In discussing the identity of Them, therefore, we must be content to take obvious facts as we find them without attempting to spin fine theories.

There are three senses in which this idea of "Them" has some foundation in fact. First, "They" may be and often are roughly conceived of as the floor traders on the Stock Exchange who are directly concerned in making quotations, pools formed to control certain stocks, or individual manipulators.

Floor traders exercise an important influence on the immediate movement of prices. Suppose, for example, they observe that offerings of Reading are very light. Declines do not induce liquidation and only small offerings of stock are met on advances. They begin to feel that, in the absence of unexpected cataclysms, Reading will not decline much. The natural thing for them to do is to begin buying Reading on all soft spots. Whenever a few hundred shares are offered at a bargain, floor traders snap up the stock.

As a result of this "bailing out" of the market, Reading becomes scarcer still, and traders, being now long, become more bullish. They begin to "mark up prices." This is not difficult, since they are, for the time being, practically unanimous in a desire for higher prices. Suppose the market is 161⅛ bid, offered at 161¼. They find that only 100 shares are for sale at ¼, and 200 are offered at ⅜. As to how much stock may be awaiting bids at ½ or higher, they cannot be sure, but can generally make a shrewd guess. One or more traders take these offerings, of perhaps 500 shares, and make the market ½ bid. The other floor traders are not willing to sell at this trifling profit, and a wait ensues to see whether any outside orders are attracted by the movement of the price, and if so, whether they are buying or selling orders. If a few buying orders come in, they are filled, perhaps at ⅝ and ¾. If selling appears, the floor traders retire in good order, take the offerings at lower prices, and try it again the next day or perhaps the next hour. Eventually, by seizing every favorable opportunity, they engineer an upward move of perhaps two or three points without taking any more stock than they want.

If such a movement attracts a following, it may easily run ten points without any real change in the prospects of the Reading road—though the prospects of the road may have had something to do with making the stock scarce before the movement started. On the other hand, if large offerings of stock are encountered at the advance, the boomlet is ignominiously squelched and the floor traders make trifling profits or losses.

Pools are not so common as most outsiders believe. There are many difficulties and complications to be overcome before a pool can be formed, held together, and operated successfully, as we had ample opportunity to observe not long ago in the case of Hocking Coal & Iron. But if a definite pool exists in any stock, its operations are practically a reproduction, on a larger scale and under a binding agreement, of the methods employed by floor traders over a smaller range and in a mere loose and voluntary association resulting from their common interests. And the individual manipulator is only a pool consisting of one person.

Second, many conceive "Them" as an association of powerful capitalists who are running a campaign in all the important speculative stocks simultaneously. It is safe to say that no such permanent and united association exists, though it would be hard to prove such a statement. But there have been many times when a single great interest was practically in control of the market for a time, other interests being content to look on, or to participate in a small way, or to await a favorable chance to take the other side.

The "Standard Oil crowd," the "Gates crowd," the "Morgan interests," and Harriman and his associates, will at once occur to the reader as having been, at various times in the past, in sole control of an important general campaign. At present the great interests are generally classified into three divisions—Morgan, Standard Oil, and Kuhn-Loeb.

A definite agreement among such interests as these would be impossible, except for limited and temporary purposes. This is perhaps not so much because these high financiers couldn't trust each other, as it is because each so-called interest consists of a loosely bound aggregation of followers of all sorts and varieties, having only one thing in common—control of capital. Such an "interest" is not an army, where the traitor can be court-martialed and shot; it is a mob, and has to be led, not driven. True, the known traitor might be put to death, financially speaking, but in stock market operations the traitor cannot, as a rule, be known. Unless his operations are of unusual size, he can successfully cover his tracks.

From this second point of view, "They" are not always active in the market. Great campaigns can only be undertaken with safety in periods when the future is to a certain extent assured. When the future is in doubt, when various confusing elements enter into the financial and political situation, leading financiers may be quite content to confine their stock market operations to individual deals, and to postpone the inauguration of a broad campaign until a more solid foundation exists for it.

Third, "They" may be conceived simply as speculators and investors in general — all that miscellaneous and heterogeneous troop of persons, scattered over the whole world, each of whom contributes his mite to the fluctuations of prices on the Stock Exchange. In this sense there is no doubt about the existence of Them, and They are the court of last resort in the establishment of prices. To put it another way, these are the "They" who are the ultimate consumers of securities. It is to Them that everybody else is planning, sooner or later, directly or indirectly, to sell his stocks.

You can lead the horse to water, but you can't make him drink. You or I or any other great millionaire can put up prices, but you can't make Them buy the stocks from you, unless They have the purchasing power and the purchasing disposition. So there is no doubt that here, at any rate, we have a conception of Them which will stand analysis without exploding.

In cases where a general campaign is being conducted, the "They" theory of values is of considerable help in the accumulation or distribution of stocks. In fact, in the late stages of a bull campaign the argument most frequently heard is likely to be something as follows: "Yes, prices are high and I can't see that future prospects are especially bullish—

but stocks are in strong hands and They will have to put them higher to make a market to sell on." Some investors make a point of dumping over all their stocks as soon as this veteran war-horse of the news brigade is groomed and trotted out. Likewise, after a prolonged bear campaign, we hear that somebody is "in trouble" and that They are going to break the market until certain concentrated holdings are brought out.

All this is very likely to be nothing but dust thrown in the eyes of that most gullible of all created beings—the haphazard speculator. When prices are so high in comparison with conditions that no sound reason can be advanced why they should go higher, a certain number of people are still induced to buy because of what They are going to do. Or, at least, if the public can no longer be induced to buy in any large volume, it is prevented from selling short for fear of what They may do.

The close student of the technical condition of the market—by which is meant the character of the long and short interests from day to day—is pretty sure to base his operations to a considerable extent on what he thinks They will do next. He has in mind Them as described in the first classification above—floor traders, pools and manipulators. He gets a good deal of help from this conception, crude as it may appear to be—largely, no doubt, because it serves to distract his mind from current news and gossip, and to prevent him from being too greatly influenced by the momentary appearance of the market.

When the market looks weakest, when the news is at the worst, when bearish prognostications are most general, is the time to buy, as every schoolboy knows; but if a man has in mind a picture of a flood of stocks pouring out from the four quarters of the globe, with no buyers, because of some desperately bad news which is just coming over the ticker, it is almost a mental impossibility for him to get up the courage to plunge in and buy. If, on the other hand, he conceives that They are just giving the market a final smash to facilitate covering a gigantic line of short stocks, he has courage to buy. His view may be right or wrong, but at least he avoids buying at the top and selling at the bottom, and he has nerve to buy a weak market and sell a strong one.

The reason for the haziness of the "They" conception in the average trader's mind is that he is only concerned with Them as They manifest Themselves through the stock market. As to who They are he feels a mild and detached curiosity; but as to Their manifestations in the market he is vitally and financially interested. It is on the latter point, therefore, that he concentrates his thoughts.

But inasmuch as definite, painstaking analysis of a situation is always better than a hazy general notion of it, the trader or investor would do much better to rid his mind of Them. The word "They" means nothing until it has an antecedent; and to use it continually without having any antecedent in mind is slipshod language, which stands for slipshod thinking. They, in the sense of the big banking interests, may be working directly against Them in the sense of individual manipulators; the manipulator, again, may be trying to trap Them in the sense of floor traders.

A genuine knowledge of the technical condition of the market cannot be summed up in any offhand declaration about what They are going to do. You cannot determine the attitude toward the market of every individual who is interested in it, but you can roughly classify the sources from which buying and selling are likely to come, the motives which are likely to actuate the various classes, and the character of the long interest and short interest. In brief, after enough study and observation, you can always have in mind some kind of an antecedent for Them, and must have it, if you base your operations on technical conditions.

IV—Confusing the Present with the Future—Discounting

IT is axiomatic that inexperienced traders and investors, and indeed a majority of the more experienced as well, are continually trying to speculate on past events. Suppose, for example, railroad earnings as published are showing constant large increases in net. The novice reasons, "Increased earnings mean increased amounts applicable to the payment of dividends. Prices should rise. I will buy."

Not at all. He should say, "Prices *have risen* to the extent represented by these increased earnings, unless this effect has been counterbalanced by other considerations. Now what next?"

It is a sort of automatic assumption of the human mind that present conditions will continue, and our whole scheme of life is necessarily based to a great degree on this assumption. When the price of wheat is high farmers increase their acreage because wheat-growing pays better; when it is low they plant less. I remember talking with a potato-raiser who claimed that he had made a good deal of money by simply reversing the above custom. When potatoes were low he had planted liberally; when high he had cut down his acreage—because he reasoned that other farmers would do just the opposite.

The average man is not blessed—or cursed, however you may look at it—with an analytical mind. We see "as through a glass darkly." Our ideas are always enveloped in a haze and our reasoning powers work in a rut from which we find it painful if not impossible to escape. Many of our emotions and some of our acts are merely automatic responses to external stimuli. Wonderful as is the development of the human brain, it originated as an enlarged ganglion, and its first response is still practically that of the ganglion.

A simple illustration of this is found in the enmity we all feel toward the alarm clock which arouses us in the morning. We have carefully set and wound that alarm and if it failed to go off it would perhaps put us to serious inconvenience; yet we reward the faithful clock with anathemas.

When a subway train is delayed nine-tenths of the people waiting on the platforms are anxiously craning their necks to see if it is coming, while many persons on it who are in danger of missing an engagement are holding themselves tense, apparently in the effort to help the train along. As a rule we apply more well-meant, but to a great extent ineffective, energy, physical or nervous, to the accomplishment of an object, than analysis or calculation.

When it comes to so complicated a matter as the price of stocks, our haziness increases in proportion to the difficulty of the subject and our ignorance of it. From reading, observation and conversation we imbibe a miscellaneous assortment of ideas from which we conclude that the situation is bullish or bearish. The very form of the expression "the situation is bullish"—not "the situation will soon become bullish"—shows the extent to which we allow the present to obscure the future in the formation of our judgment.

Catch any trader and pin him down to it and he will readily admit that the logical moment for the highest prices is when the news is most bullish; yet you will find him buying stocks on this news after it comes out—if not at the moment, at any rate "on a reaction."

Most coming events cast their shadows before, and it is on this that intelligent speculation must be based. The movement of prices in anticipation of such an event is called "discounting," and this process of discounting is worthy a little careful examination.

The first point to be borne in mind is that some events cannot be discounted, even by the supposed omniscience of the great banking interests—which is in point of fact, more than half imaginary. The San Francisco earthquake is the standard example of an event which could not be foreseen and therefore could not be discounted; but an event does not have to be purely an "act of God" to be undiscountable. There can be no question that our great bankers have been as much in the dark in regard to some recent Supreme Court decisions as the smallest "piker" in the customers' room of an odd-lot brokerage house.

If the effect of an event does not make itself felt before the event takes place, it must come after. In all discussion of discounting we must bear this fact in mind in order that our subject may not run away with us.

On the other hand an event may sometimes be overdiscounted. If the dividend rate on a stock is to be raised from four to five per cent., earnest bulls, with an eye to their own commitments, may spread rumors of six or seven per cent., so that the actual declaration of five per cent. may be received as disappointing and cause a decline.

Generally speaking, every event which is under the control of capitalists associated with the property, or any financial condition which is subject to the management of combined banking interests, is likely to be pretty thoroughly discounted before it occurs. There is never any lack of capital to take advantage of a sure thing, even though it may be known in advance to only a few persons.

The extent to which future business conditions are known to "insiders" is, however, usually overestimated. So much depends, especially in America, upon the size of the crops, the temper of the people, and the policies adopted by leading politicians, that the future of business becomes a very complicated problem. No power can drive the American people. Any control over their action has to be exercised by cajolery or by devious and circuitous methods.

Moreover, public opinion is becoming

more volatile and changeable year by year, owing to the quicker spread of information and the rapid multiplication of the reading public. One can easily imagine that some of our older financiers must be saying to themselves, "If I had only had my present capital in 1870, or else had the conditions of 1870 to work on today!"

A fair idea of when the discounting process will be completed may usually be formed by studying conditions from every angle. The great question is, when will the buying or selling become most general and urgent? In 1907, for example, the safest and best time to buy the sound dividend-paying stocks was on the Monday following the bank statement which showed the greatest decrease in reserves. The markets opened down several points under pressure of liquidation, and standard issues never sold so low afterward. The simple explanation was that conditions had become so bad that they could not get any worse without utter ruin, which all parties must and did unite to prevent.

Likewise in the Presidential campaign of 1900, the lowest prices were made on Bryan's nomination. Everyone said at once, "He can't be elected." Therefore his nomination was the worst that could happen—the point of time where the political news became most intensely bearish. As the campaign developed his defeat became more and more certain, and prices continued to rise in accordance with the general economic and financial conditions of the period.

It is not the discounting of an event thus known in advance to capitalists, that presents the greatest difficulties, but cases where considerable uncertainty exists, so that even the clearest mind and the most accurate information can result only in a balancing of probabilities, with the scale perhaps inclined to a greater or less degree in one direction or the other.

In some cases the uncertainty which precedes such an event is more depressing than the worst that can happen afterward. An example is a Supreme Court decision upon a previously undetermined public policy which has kept business men so much in the dark that they feared to go ahead with any important plans. This was the case at the time of the Northern Securities decision in 1904. "Big business" could easily enough adjust itself to either result. It was the uncertainty that was bearish. Hence the decision was practically discounted in advance, no matter what it might prove to be.

This was not true to the same extent of the Standard Oil and American Tobacco decisions of 1911, because those decisions were an earnest of more trouble to come. The decisions were greeted by a temporary spurt of activity, based on the theory that the removal of uncertainty was the important thing; but a sensational decline started soon after and was not checked until the announcement that the Government would prosecute the United States Steel Corporation. This was deemed the worst that could happen for some time to come, and was followed by a considerable advance.

More commonly, when an event is uncertain the market estimates the chances with considerable nicety. Each trader backs his own opinion, strongly if he feels confident, moderately if he still has a few doubts which he cannot down. The result of these opposing views may be stationary prices, or a market fluctuating nervously within a narrow range, or a movement in either direction, greater or smaller in proportion to the more or less emphatic preponderance of the buying or selling.

Of course it must always be remembered that it is the dollars that count, not the number of buyers or sellers. A few great capitalists having advance information which they regard as accurate, may more than counterbalance thousands of small traders who hold an opposite opinion. In fact, this is a condition very frequently seen, as explained in a previous chapter.

Even the operations of an individual

investor usually have an effect on prices pretty accurately adjusted to his opinions. When he believes prices are low and everything favors an upward movement, he will strain his resources in order to accumulate as heavy a load of securities as he can carry. After a fair advance, if he sees the development of some factor which *might* cause a decline —though he doesn't really believe it will —he thinks it wise to lighten his load somewhat and make sure of some of his accumulated profits. Later when he feels that prices are "high enough," he is a liberal seller; and if some danger appears while the level of quoted values continues high, he "cleans house," to be ready for whatever may come. Then if what he considers an unwarranted speculation carries prices still higher, he is very likely to sell a few hundred shares short by way of occupying his capital and his mind.

It is, however, the variation of opinion among different men that has the largest influence in making the market responsive to changing conditions. A development which causes one trader to lighten his line of stocks may be regarded as harmless or even beneficial by another, so that he maintains his position or perhaps buys more. Out of a world-wide mixture of varying ideas, personalities and information emerges the average level of prices—the true index number of investment conditions.

The necessary result of the above line of reasoning is that not only probabilities but even rather remote possibilities are reflected in the market. Hardly any event can happen of sufficient importance to attract general attention which some process of reasoning cannot construe as bullish and some other process interpret as bearish. Doubtless even our old friend of the news columns to the effect that "the necessary activities of a nation of ninety million souls create and maintain a large volume of business," may influence some red-blooded optimist to buy 100 Union; but the grouchy pessimist who has eaten too many doughnuts for breakfast will accept the statement as an evidence of the scarcity of real bull news and will likely enough sell 100 Union short on the strength of it.

It is the overextended speculator who causes most of the fluctuations that look absurd to the sober observer. It does not take much to make a man buy when he is short of stocks "up to his neck." A bit of news which he would regard as insignificant at any other time will then assume an exaggerated importance in his eyes. His fears increase in geometrical proportion to the size of his line of stocks. Likewise the overloaded bull may begin to "throw his stocks" on some absurd story of a war between Honduras and Roumania, without even stopping to look up the geographical location of the countries involved.

Fluctuations based on absurdities are always relatively small. They are due to an exaggerated fear of what "the other fellow" may do. Personally, you do not fear a war between Honduras and Roumania; but may not the rumor be seized upon by the bears as an excuse for a raid? And you have too many stocks to be comfortable if such a break should occur. Moreover, even if the bears do not raid the market, will there not be a considerable number of persons who, like yourself, will fear such a raid, and will therefore lighten their load of stocks, thus causing some decline?

The professional trader, following this line of reasoning to the limit, eventually comes to base all his operations for short turns in the market not on the facts but on what he believes the facts will cause others to do—or more accurately, perhaps, on what he *sees* that the news *is* causing others to do; for such a trader is likely to keep his finger constantly on the pulse of buying and selling as it throbs on the floor of the Exchange or as recorded on the tape.

The non-professional, however, will do well not to let his mind stray too far into the unknown territory of what others may do. Like the "They" theory of values, it is dangerous ground in that it leads toward the abdication of common sense; and after all, others may not prove to be such fools as we think they are. While the market is likely to discount even a possibility, the chances are very much against *our* being able to discount the possibility profitably.

In this matter of discounting, as in connection with most other stock market phenomena, the most useful hint that can be given is to avoid all efforts to reduce the movement of prices to rules, measures, or similarities and to analyze each case by itself. Historical parallels are likely to be misleading. Every situation is new, though usually composed of familiar elements. Each element must be weighed by itself and the probable result of the combination estimated. In most cases the problem is by no means impossible, but the student must learn to look into the future and to consider the present only as a guide to the future. Extreme prices will come at the time when the news is most emphatic and most widely disseminated. When that point is passed the question must always be, "What next?"

V—Confusing the Personal with the General

IN a previous chapter the fact has been mentioned that one of the greatest difficulties encountered by the active trader is that of keeping his mind in a balanced and unprejudiced condition when he is heavily committed to either the long or short side of the market. Unconsciously to himself, he permits his judgment to be swayed by his hopes.

A former large speculator on the Chicago Board of Trade, after being short of the market and very bearish on wheat for a long time, one day surprised all his friends by covering everything, going long a moderate amount, and arguing violently on the bull side. For two days he maintained this position, but the market failed to go up. He then turned back to the short side, and had even more bear arguments at his tongue's end than before.

To a certain extent he did this to test the market, but still more to test himself—to see whether, by changing front and taking the other side, he could persuade himself out of his bearish opinions. When even this failed to make any real change in his views, he was reassured and was ready for a new and more aggressive campaign on the short side.

There is nothing peculiar about this condition. While it is especially difficult to maintain a balanced mind in regard to commitments in the markets, it is not easy to do so about anything that closely touches our personal interests. As a rule we can find plenty of reasons for doing what we very much want to do, and we are still more prolific with excuses for not doing what we don't want to do. Most of us change the old sophism "Whatever is, is right" to the more directly useful form "Whatever I want is right." To many readers will occur at once the name of a man prominent in public life who seems very frequently to act on this motto.

If Smith and Jones have a verbal agreement, which afterwards turns out to be greatly to Jones' advantage, Smith's recollection is that it was merely a loose understanding which could be cancelled at any time, while Jones remembers it to have been a definite legal contract, perfectly enforceable if it had only been written. Talleyrand said that language was given us for the purpose of concealing thought. Likewise many seem to think that logic was given us for the purpose of backing up our desires.

Few persons are so introspective as to be able to tell where this bias in favor of their own interests begins and where it leaves off. Still fewer bother to make the effort to tell. To a great extent we train our judgment to lend itself to our selfish interests. The question with us is not so much whether we have the facts of a situation correctly in mind, as whether we can "put it over."

When it comes to buying and selling stocks, there is no such thing as "putting it over." The market is relentless. It cannot be budged by our sophistries. It will respond exactly to the forces and personalities which are working upon it, with no more regard for our opinions than if we couldn't vote. We cannot work for our own interests as in other lines of business—we can only fit our interests to the facts.

To make the greatest success it is necessary for the trader to forget entirely his own position *in* the market, his profits or losses, the relation of present prices to the point where he bought or sold, and to fix his thoughts upon the position *of* the market. If the market is going down the trader must sell, no matter whether he has a profit or a loss, whether he bought a year ago or two minutes ago.

How far the average trader is from attaining this point of view is quickly seen from his conversation, and it is also true that a great deal of the literature of speculation absolutely fails to reach this conception.

"You have five points profit—you had better take it," advises the broker. Perhaps so, if you know nothing about the market; but if you understand the market the time to take your profit is when the upward movement shows signs of culminating, regardless of your own deal.

"Stop your losses; let your profits run" is a saying which appeals to the novice as the essence of wisdom. But the whole question is *where* to stop the losses and *how far* to let the profits run. In other words, what is the *market* going to do? If you can tell this your personal losses and profits will take care of themselves.

Here is a man who has done a great deal of figuring and has proved to his own satisfaction that seven points is the correct profit to take in Union Pacific, while losses should be limited to two and one-half points. Nothing could be more foolish than these arbitrary figures. He is trying to make the market fit itself around his own trades, instead of adapting his trades to the market.

In any broker's office you will notice that a large part of the talk concerns the profits and losses of the traders. Brown had a profit of ten points and then let it get away from him. "Great Scott!" says his wise friend. "What do you want? Aren't you satisfied with ten points profit?" The reply should be, though it rarely is, "Certainly not, if I think the market is going higher."

"Get them out with a small profit," I once heard one broker say to another. "If you don't they will hang on and take a loss. They never get profit enough to satisfy them." A good policy, probably, if neither the broker nor his customer had any real knowledge of the market; but mere nonsense for the trader who aims to be in the slightest degree scientific.

The fact is that the more a trader allows his mind to dwell upon his own position in the market the more likely it is that his judgment will become warped so that his mind is blind to those considerations which do not fall in with his preconceived opinion.

Until you try it, you have almost no idea of the extent to which you may be rendered unreasonable by the mere fact that you are committed to one side of the market. "In the market, to be consistent is to be stubborn," some one has said; and it is true that the man of strong will and logical intellect is often less successful than the more shallow and volatile observer, who is ready to whiffle about like the weathercock at any suspicion of a change in the wind. This is because the strong man has in this instance embarked upon an enterprise where he cannot use his natural force and determination—he can employ only his faculties of observation and interpretation. Yet in the end the man of character will be the more permanently successful, because he will eventually master his subject more thoroughly and attain a more judicial attitude.

The more simple-minded, after once committing themselves to a position, are thereafter chiefly influenced and supported by the illusions of hope. They bought, probably, as a result of some bullish development. If prices have advanced, they find that the market "looks strong," a good deal of encouraging news comes out on the tickers, and they hope for large profits. After five points in their favor, they hope for ten, and after ten they look for fifteen or twenty.

On the other hand, if prices decline they charge it to "manipulation," "bear raids," etc., and expect an early recovery. Much of the bear news appears to them to be put out maliciously, in order to cause prices to decline further. It is not until the decline begins to cause a painful encroachment upon their capital that they reach the point of saying, "If 'they' can depress prices like this in the face of a bullish situation, what is the use of fighting them? By a flood of short sales, they can put prices down as much as they like"— or something of the sort.

Such traders are suffering merely from youth, or lack of sound business sense, or both. They have a considerable period of study before them, if they persist until they get permanently profitable results. Most of them, of course, do not persist.

A much more intelligent class, many of whom are properly to be considered as investors, do not allow their position in the market to blind them so far as current news or statistical developments are concerned, but do permit themselves to become biased in regard to the most important factor of all— the effect of a change in the price level.

They bought stocks in the expectation of an improved situation. The improved situation comes and prices rise. Nothing serious in the way of bear news appears. On the contrary, bull news continues plentiful.

Under these conditions they see no reason for selling.

Yet there may be a most important reason for selling—namely, that prices have risen sufficiently to counterbalance the improved situation—and they would see and appreciate this fact if they were in the position of an uninterested observer.

One of the principal reasons why investors of this class allow themselves to become confused as to the influence of the price level is because a bull market nearly always goes unreasonably high before it culminates. The investor has perhaps, in several previous instances, sold out at what he thought was a fair price level, only to see the public run away with the market to a point where his profits would have been doubled if he had held on.

It is in such cases that an expert knowledge of speculation is essential. If the investor has not this knowledge, and cannot obtain the dependable advice of one who has it, then he must content himself with more moderate profits and forego the expectation of getting the full benefit of the advance. But with a fair knowledge of speculative influences, he can fix his mind on the development of the campaign, regardless of his own holdings, and can usually secure a larger profit than if he depended merely upon ordinary business "common sense."

The mistake is made when, without any expert knowledge of speculation, he permits himself to hold on in the hope of higher prices after a level has been reached which has fairly discounted improved business conditions.

Not one trader in a thousand ever becomes so expert or so seasoned as to entirely overcome the influence his position in the market exerts upon his judgment. That influence appears in the most insidious and elusive ways. One of the principal difficulties of the expert is in preventing his active imagination from causing him to see what he is looking for just because he is looking for it.

An example will make this clear.

The expert has learned from experience, let us say, that the appearance of "holes" in the market is a sign of weakness. By a "hole" is meant a condition of the market where it suddenly and unaccountably refuses to take stock. A few hundred shares of an active stock are offered for sale. Sentiment is generally bullish, but there is no buyer for that stock. Prices slip quickly down half a point or a point before buyers are found. This, in an active stock, is unusual; and although the price may recover, the professional does not forget this treacherous failure of the market to accept moderate offerings. He considers it a sign of an "over-bought" market.

Now suppose the trader has calculated that an advance is about to culminate and has taken the short side in anticipation of that event. He suspects that the market is over-bought, but is not yet sure of it. Under these circumstances any little dip in the price will perhaps look to him like a "hole," even though under other conditions he would not notice it or would think nothing about it. He is looking for the development of weakness and there is danger that his imagination may show him what he is looking for even though it isn't there!

The same remarks would apply to the detection of accumulation or distribution. If you want to see distribution after a sharp advance, you are very likely to see it. If you have sold out and want to get a reaction on which to repurchase, you will see plenty of indications of a reaction. Indeed, it is a sort of proverb in Wall Street that there is no bear so bearish as a sold-out bull who wants a chance to repurchase.

In the study of so-called "technical" conditions of the market, a situation often appears which permits a double construction. Indications of various kinds are almost evenly balanced; some things might be interpreted in two different ways; and a trader not already interested in the market would be likely to think it wise to stay out until he could see his way more clearly.

Under such circumstances you will find it an almost invariable rule that the man who was long before this condition arose will interpret technical conditions as bullish, while the man who was and remains short, sees plain indications of technical weakness. Somewhat amusing, but true.

In this matter of allowing the judgment to be influenced by personal commitments, very little of a constructive or practically helpful nature can be written, except the one word "Don't." Yet when the investor or trader has come to realize that he is a prejudiced observer, he has made progress; for this knowledge keeps him from trusting too blindly to something which, at the moment, he calls judgment, but which may turn out to be simply an unusually strong impulse of greed.

It has often been noted by stock market writers that since the great public is bearish at the bottom and bullish at the top, it could make its fortune and beat the multi-millionaires at their own game by simply reversing itself—buying when it feels like selling and selling when it feels like buying. Tom Lawson, in the heyday of his publicity, seems to have had some sort of dream of the public selling back to Standard Oil capitalists the stocks which it had bought from them and thus bringing everything to smash in a heap—the philanthropic Thomas, doubtless, being first properly short of the market.

This wrongheadedness of the public no longer exists to the same extent as formerly. A great number of small investors buy and sell intelligently and there has been a most noticeable falling off in the gambling class of trade—much to the satisfaction of everyone, except, perhaps, the brokers who formerly handled such business.

It remains true, nevertheless, that the very moment when the market looks strongest, is likely to be near the top, and just when prices appear to have started on a straight drop to the zero point is usually near the bottom

The practical way for the investor to use this principle is to be ready to sell at the moment when bull sentiment seems to be most widely distributed, and to buy when the public in general seem most discouraged. It is especially important for him to bear this principle in mind in taking profits on previous commitments, as his own interests are then identified with the current trend of prices.

In a word, the trader or investor who has studied the subject enough to be reading this book, probably could not make profits by reversing himself, even if such a thing were possible; but he can endeavor to hold himself in a detached, unprejudiced frame of mind, and to study the psychology of the crowd, especially as it manifests itself in the movement of prices.

VI—The Panic and the Boom

BOTH the panic and the boom are eminently psychological phenomena. This is not saying that fundamental conditions do not at times warrant sharp declines in prices and at other times equally sharp advances. But the panic, properly so-called, represents a decline greater than is warranted by conditions, usually because of an excited state of the public mind, accompanied by exhaustion of resources; while the term "boom" is used to mean an excessive and largely speculative advance.

There are some special features connected with the panic and the boom which are worthy of separate consideration.

It is really astonishing what a hold the fear of a possible panic has upon the minds of many investors. The memory of the events of 1907 has undoubtedly operated greatly to lessen the volume of speculative trade from that time to the present (April, 1912). Panics of equal severity have occurred only a few times in the entire history of the country, and the possibility of such an outbreak in any one month is smaller than the chance of loss on the average investment through the failure of the company. Yet the specter of such a panic rises in the minds of the inexperienced whenever they think of buying stocks.

"Yes," the investor may say, "Reading seems to be in a very strong position, but look where it sold in 1907—at $70 a share!"

It is sometimes assumed that the low prices in a panic are due to a sudden spasm of fear, which comes quickly and passes away quickly. This is not the case. In a way, the operation of the element of fear begins when prices are near the top. Some cautious investors begin to fear that the boom is being overdone and that a disastrous decline must follow the excessive speculation for the rise. They sell under the influence of this feeling.

During the ensuing decline, which may run for years, more and more people begin to feel uneasy over business or financial conditions, and they liquidate their holdings. This caution or fearfulness gradually spreads, increasing and decreasing in waves, but growing a little greater at each successive swell. The panic is not a sudden development, but is the result of causes long accumulated.

The actual bottom prices of the panic are more likely to result from necessity than from fear. Those investors who could be frightened out of their holdings are likely to give up before the bottom is reached. The lowest prices are usually made by sales for those whose immediate resources are exhausted. Most of them are taken by surprise and could raise the money necessary to carry their stocks if they had a little time; but in the stock market, "time is the essence of the contract," and is the very thing that they cannot have.

The great cause of loss in times of panic is the failure of the investor to keep enough of his capital in liquid form. He becomes "tied up" in various undertakings so that he cannot realize quickly. He may have abundant property, but no ready money. This condition, in turn, results from trying to do too much—greed, haste, excessive ambition, an oversupply of easy confidence as to the future.

It is noticeable in panic times that a period arrives when nearly every one thinks that stocks are low enough, yet prices continue downward to a still lower level. The result is that many investors, after thinking that they have "loaded up" near the bottom, find that it was a false bottom, and are finally forced to throw over their holdings on a further decline.

This is due to the fact mentioned

above, that final low prices are the result of necessities, not of opinions. In 1907, for example, every one of good sense knew perfectly well that stocks were selling below their value—the trouble was that investors could not get hold of the money with which to buy.

The moral is that low prices, after a prolonged bear period, are not in themselves a sufficient reason for buying stocks. The key to the situation lies in the *accumulation of liquid capital,* which is most quickly evidenced by a rapid recovery of the excess of deposits over loans in the New York clearing house banks (excluding the trust companies, in which loans are more varied). This subject, however, takes us outside our present field.

It is to a great extent because the last part of the decline in a panic has been caused not by public opinion, or even by public fear, but by necessity, arising from absolute exhaustion of available funds, that the first part of the ensuing recovery takes place without any apparent reason.

Traders say, "The panic is over, but stocks cannot go up much under such bearish conditions as now exist." Yet stocks can and do go up, because they are merely regaining the natural level from which they were depressed by "bankrupt sales," as we would say in discussing dry goods.

Perhaps the word "fear" has been overworked in the discussion of stock market psychology. It is only the very few who actually sell their stocks under the direct influence of the emotion of fear. But a feeling of caution strong enough to induce sales, or even a fixed belief that prices must decline, constitutes in itself a sort of modification of fear, and has the same result so far as prices are concerned.

The effect of this fear or caution in a panic is not limited to the selling of stocks, but is even more important in preventing purchases. It takes far less uneasiness to cause the intending investor to delay purchases than to precipitate actual sales by holders. For this reason, a small quantity of stock pressed for sale in a panicky market may cause a decline out of all proportion to its importance. The offerings may be small, but nobody wants them.

It is this factor which accounts for the rapid recoveries which frequently follow panics. Waiting investors are afraid to step in front of a demoralized market, but once the turn appears, they fall over each other to buy.

The boom is in many ways the reverse of the panic. Just as fear keeps growing and spreading until the final crash, so confidence and enthusiasm keep reproducing each other on a wider and wider scale until the result is a sort of hilarity on the part of thousands of men, many of them comparatively young and inexperienced, who have "made big money" during the long advance in prices.

These imaginary millionaires appear in a small swarm during every prolonged bull market, only to fall with their wings singed as soon as prices decline. Such speculators are, to all practical intents and purposes, irresponsible. It is their very irresponsibility which has enabled them to make money so rapidly on advancing prices. The prudent man gets only moderate profits in a bull market—it is the man who trades on "shoe-string margins" who gets the biggest benefit out of the rise.

When such mushroom fortunes have accumulated, the market may fall temporarily into the hands of these daredevil spirits, so that almost any recklessness is possible for the time. It is this kind of buying which causes prices to go higher after they are already high enough—just as they go lower in a panic after they are plainly seen to be low enough.

When prices get above the natural level, a well-judged short interest begins to appear. These shorts are right, but right too soon. In a genuine bull market they are nearly always driven to cover by a further rise, which is, from any common sense standpoint, unreasonable. A riot of pyramided margins drives the sane and calculating short seller temporarily to shelter.

A psychological influence of a much wider scope also operates to help a bull market along to unreasonable heights. Such a market is usually accompanied by rising prices in all lines of business and these rising prices always create, in the minds of business men, the impression that their various enterprises are more profitable than is really the case.

One reason for this false impression is found in stocks of goods on hand. Take the wholesale grocer, for example, carrying a stock of goods which inventories $10,000 in January, 1909. On that date Bradstreet's index of commodity prices stood at 8.26. In January, 1910, Bradstreet's index was 9.23. If the prices of the various articles included in this stock of groceries increased in the same ratio as Bradstreet's list, and if the grocer had on hand exactly the same things, he would inventory them at about $11,168 in January, 1910.

He made an additional profit of $1,168 during the year without any effort, and probably without any calculation, on his part. But this profit was only apparent, not real; for he could not buy any more with the $11,168 in January, 1910, than he could have bought with the $10,000 in January, 1909. He is deceived into supposing himself richer than he really is, and this false idea leads to a gradual growth of extravagance and speculation in every line of business and every walk of life.

The secondary results of this delusion of increased wealth because of rising prices, are even more important than the primary results. Our grocer, for example, decides to spend this $1,168 for an automobile. This helps the automobile business. Hundreds of similar orders induce the automobile company to enlarge its plant. This means extensive purchases of material and employment of labor. The increased demand resulting from a similar condition of things in all departments of industry produces, if other conditions are favorable, a still further rise in prices; hence at the end of another year the grocer perhaps has another imaginary profit, which he spends in enlarging his residence or buying new furniture, etc.

The stock market feels the reflection of all this increased business and higher prices. Yet the whole thing is psychological, and sooner or later our grocer must earn and save, by hard work, economical living and shrewd calculation, the amount he has paid for his automobile or furniture.

Again, rising stock prices and rising commodity prices react on each other. If the grocer, in addition to his imaginary profit of $1,168 sees a ten per cent. advance in the prices of various securities which he holds for investment, he is encouraged to still larger expenditures; and likewise if the capitalist notes a ten per cent. advance in the stock market, he perhaps employs additional servants and enlarges his household expenditures so that he buys more groceries. Thus the feeling of confidence and enthusiasm spreads wider and wider like ripples from a stone dropped into a pond. And all of these developments are faithfully reflected by the stock market barometer.

The result is that, in a year like 1902 or 1906, the high prices for stocks and the feverish activity of general trade are based, to an entirely unsuspected extent, on a sort of pyramid of mistaken impressions, most of which may be traced, directly or indirectly, to the fact that we measure everything in money and always think of this money-measure as fixed and unchangeable, while in reality our money fluctuates in value just like iron, potatoes, or "Fruit of the Loom." We are accustomed to figuring the money-value of wheat, but we get a headache when we try to reckon the wheat-value of money.

When a fictitious situation like this begins to go to pieces, the stock market, fulfilling its function of barometer, declines first, while general business continues active. Then the "money sharks of Wall Street" get themselves roundly cursed by the public and there is a widespread desire to wipe them off the earth in summary fashion. The stock market never finds itself popular unless it is going up; yet its going down undoubtedly does far more to promote the country's welfare in the long run, for it serves to temper the crash which must eventually come in general business circles and to forewarn us of trouble ahead so that we may prepare for it.

It is generally more difficult to distinguish the end of a stock market boom than to decide when a panic is definitely over. The principle of the thing is simple enough, however. It was an oversupply of liquid capital that started the market upward after the panic was over. Similarly it is exhaustion of liquid capital which brings the bull movement to an end. This exhaustion is shown by higher call money rates, loss of the excess of deposits over loans in New York clearinghouse banks, a steady rise in commercial paper rates, and a sagging market for high-grade bonds.

VII—The Psychology of Scale Orders

THE observer of market conditions soon comes to know that there are two general classes of minds whose operations are reflected in prices. These classes might be named the "impulsive" and the "phlegmatic."

The "impulsive" operator says, for example, "Conditions, both fundamental and technical, warrant higher prices. Stocks are a purchase." Having formed this conclusion, he proceeds to buy. He does not try or expect to buy at the bottom. On the contrary he is perfectly willing to buy at the top so far, provided he sees prospects of a further advance. When he concludes that conditions have turned bearish, or that the advance in prices has overdiscounted previous conditions, he sells out.

The "phlegmatic" type of investor,

on the other hand, can hardly ever be persuaded to buy on an advance. He reasons, "Prices frequently move several points against conditions, or at least against what the conditions seem to me to be. The sensible thing for me to do is to take advantage of these contrary movements."

Hence when he believes stocks should be bought he places an order to buy on a scale. His thought is:

"It seems to me stocks should advance from these prices, but I am not a soothsayer, and prices have often declined three points when I felt just as bullish as I do now. So I will place orders to buy every half point down for three points. These speculators are a crazy lot and there is no knowing what passing breeze might strike them that would cause a temporary decline of a few points."

Among large capitalists, and especially in the banking community, the "phlegmatic" type naturally predominates. Such men have neither the time nor the disposition to watch the ticker closely and they nearly always disclaim any ability to predict the smaller movements of prices. They are entirely ready, nevertheless, to take advantage of these small fluctuations when they occur, and having plenty of capital, they can easily accomplish this by buying or selling on a scale.

As a matter of fact, the market is usually full of scale orders, and the knowledge of this and of the way in which such orders are handled is decidedly helpful in judging the tone and technical position of the market from day to day.

The two types of operators above described are always working against each other. The buying or selling of the "impulsive" trader tends to force prices up or down, while the scale orders of the "phlegmatic" class tend to oppose any movement.

For example, let us suppose that banking interests believe conditions to be fundamentally sound and that the general trend of the market will be upward for some time to come. Orders are therefore placed by various persons to buy stocks every point down, or every half, quarter, or even eighth point down.

On the other hand, the active floor traders find that, owing to some temporary unfavorable development, a following can be obtained on the bear side. They perceive the presence of scale orders, but they think stocks enough will come out on the decline to fill the scale orders and leave a balance over.

To put it another way, the floating supply of stocks has become, at the moment, larger than can comfortably be tossed about from hand to hand by the in-and-out class of traders. The market must decline until a part of this floating supply is absorbed by the scale orders which underlie current prices.

These conditions produce what is commonly called a "reaction." Once this surplus floating supply of stocks is absorbed by standing orders, the market is ready to start upward again. If the general trend is upward, far less resistance will be encountered on the advance than was met on the reaction; hence prices rise to a new high level. Then profit-taking sales will be met, on limited or scale orders at various prices, and as the market advances the floating supply will gradually increase until it again becomes unwieldy and another reaction is necessary.

Eventually a level is reached, or some change in conditions appears, which causes these scale buying orders to be partially or entirely withdrawn, and selling orders to be substituted on a scale up. The bull market will not go much further after this change takes place. It has now become easier to produce declines than advances. The situation is the reverse of that described above, and a bear market follows.

Commonly there is a considerable period around top prices when scale buying orders are still found on declines, but profit-taking sales are also met on advances, so that the market is kept fluctuating within comparatively narrow limits for a month or more. In fact, it is likely to be kept on this level so long as public buying continues greater than public selling. This is sometimes called "distribution." A similar period of "accumulation" often occurs after a bear market has run its course, and before any important advance appears.

A close watch of transactions, or a study of continuous quotations as published in certain newspapers, often enables the experienced trader to discover when the most important of these scale orders are withdrawn or reversed.

A bull market which is full of scale buying orders encounters "support," so-called, on declines. Bears are timid about driving down prices, because they are continually "losing their stocks." They say that "very little stock comes out on declines"; hence there is a certain appearance of caution in the way the market goes down, and the activity of trade shows, in a broad way, a falling off at lower prices. On the advances, however, a following is obtained and activity increases.

Toward the end of the bull market a change is noticeable. Prices go down easily and on larger transactions, while advances are sluggish and opposition is met at higher levels where profit-taking orders have been placed. The very day when scale buying orders in a stock are withdrawn can oftentimes be distinguished.

In a bear market, "pressure" appears in place of "support." The scale orders are mostly to sell as the market rises. Only a small following of purchasers is obtainable on advances, hence the activity of business, in a general way, falls off as prices go up. The end of the bear market is marked by the reappearance of "support" and the removal of "pressure," so that prices rebound quickly and sharply from declines.

The common assumption is that this

"support" or "pressure" is supplied by "manipulators." But it is quite as likely to result from the scale operations of hundreds of different persons, whose mental make-up prevents them from buying or selling in the "impulsive" way.

VIII—The Mental Attitude of the Individual

IN previous chapters we have seen that many, if not most, of the eccentricities of speculative markets, commonly charged to manipulation, are in fact due to the peculiar psychological conditions which surround such markets. Especially, and more than all else together, these erratic fluctuations are the result of the efforts of traders to operate, not on the basis of facts, nor on their own judgment as to the effect of facts on prices, but on what they believe will be the probable effect of facts or rumors on the minds of other traders. This mental attitude opens up a broad field of conjecture, which is not limited by any definite boundaries of fact or common sense.

Yet it would be foolish to assert that assuming a position in the market based on what others will do is a wrong attitude. It is confusing to the uninitiated, and first efforts to work on such a plan are almost certain to be disastrous; but for the experienced it becomes a successful, though of course never a certain, method. A child's first efforts to use a sharp tool are likely to result in bloodshed, but the same tool may trace an exquisite carving in the hands of an expert.

What, then, should be the mental attitude of the intelligent buyer and seller of securities?

The "long pull" investor, buying outright for cash and holding for a liberal profit, need only consider this matter enough to guard against becoming confused by the vagaries of public sentiment or by his own inverted reasoning processes. He will get the best results by keeping his eye single to two things: Facts and Prices. The current rate of interest, the earning power of the corporations whose stocks he buys, the development of political conditions as affecting invested capital, and the relation of current prices to the situation as shown by these three factors—these constitute the most important food for his mind to work upon.

When he finds himself wandering off into a consideration of what "They" will do next, or what effect such and such events may have on the sentiment of speculators, he cannot do better than to bring himself up with a short turn and sternly bid himself "Back to common sense."

For the more active trader the situation is different. He need not be entirely unregardful of values or fundamental conditions, but his prime object is to "go with the tide." That means basing his operations to a great extent on what others will think and do. His own mental attitute, then, is a most important part of his equipment for success.

First, the trader must be a *reasoning optimist*. A more horrible fate can scarcely be imagined than the shallow pessimism of many market habitués, whose minds, incapable of grasping the larger forces beneath the movements of prices, take refuge in a cynical disbelief in pretty much everything that makes life worth living.

Owing to the nature of the business, however, this optimism must be of a somewhat different character from that which brings success in other lines. As a general thing optimism includes the persistent nourishing of hope, an aggressive confidence, the certainty that you are right, a firm determination to accomplish your end. But you cannot make the stock market move your way by believing that it will do so. Here is one case, at any rate, where New Thought methods cannot be directly applied.

In the market you are nothing but a chip on the tide of events. Optimism, then, must consist in believing, not that the tide will continually flow your way, but that you will succeed in floating with the tide. Your optimism must be, in a sense, of the intellect, not of the will. An optimism based on determination would, in this case, amount to stubbornness.

Another quality that makes for success in nearly every line of business is enthusiasm. For this you have absolutely no use in the stock market. The moment you permit yourself to become enthusiastic, you are subordinating your reasoning powers to your beliefs or desires.

Enthusiasm helps you influence other men's minds, but in the market you do not desire to do this (unless you happen to be a big bull leader). You wish to keep your mind as clear, cool and unruffled as the surface of a mountain lake on a calm day. Any emotion—enthusiasm, fear, anger, depression—will only cloud the intellect.

Doubtless it would be axiomatic to warn the trader against stubbornness. It cannot be assumed that any operator would consciously permit himself to become stubborn. The trouble arises in drawing the line between, on the one hand, persistence, consistence, pursuit of a definite plan until conditions change; and, on the other, stubborn adherence to a course of action which subsequent events have proved to be erroneous.

A day in the country, with the market forgotten, or if necessary forcibly ejected from the thoughts, will often enable the trader to return with a clarified mind, so that he can then intelligently convict or acquit himself of the vice of stubbornness. Sometimes it may become necessary to close all commitments and remain out of the market for a few days.

One of the most common errors might be described as "getting a notion." This is due to the failure or inability of the trader to take a broad view of the entire situation. Some particular point in the complex conditions which usually control prices, appeals to him strongly and impresses him as certain to have its effect on the market. He acts on this single idea. The idea may be all right, but other counterbalancing factors may prevent it from having its natural effect.

You encounter these "notions" every day in the Street. You meet a highly conservative individual and ask him what he thinks of the situation. "I am alarmed at the rapid spread of radical sentiment," he replies. "How can we expect capital to branch out into new enterprises when the profits may be swept away at any moment by socialistic legislation?"

You say mildly that the crops are good, the banking situation sound, business active, etc. But all this produces no impression upon him. He has sold all his stocks and has his money in the banks. (He is also short a considerable line, but he doesn't tell you this). He will not buy again until the public becomes "sane."

The next man you talk with says: "We cannot have much decline with the present good crop prospect. Crops lie at the basis of everything. With nine billions of new wealth coming out of the ground and flowing into the channels of trade, we are bound to have prosperous conditions for some time to come."

You speak of radicalism, adverse legislation, high cost of living, etc.; but he thinks these are relatively unimportant compared with that $9,000,000,000 of new wealth. Of course, he is long of stocks.

"To make the worse appear the better reason," said Mr. Socrates, some little time ago. It is too bad we can't have Socrates' comments on Wall Street. The Socratic method applied to the average speculator would produce amusing results.

Beware of saying, "This is the most important factor in the situation," unless the action of the market shows that others agree with you. Every human mind has its own peculiarities, so presumably yours has, though you can't see them plainly; but the stock market is the meeting of many minds, having every imaginable peculiarity.

However important some single factor in the situation may appear to you, it is not going to control the movement of prices regardless of everything else.

An exaggerated example of "getting a notion" is seen in the so-called "hunch." This term appears to mean, when it means anything, a sort of sudden welling up of instinct so strong as to induce the trader to follow it regardless of reason. In many cases, the "hunch" is nothing more than a strong impulse.

Almost any business man will say at times, "I have a feeling that we ought not to do this," or "Somehow I don't like that proposition," without being able to explain clearly the grounds for his opposition. Likewise the "hunch" of a man who has watched the stock market for half a lifetime may not be without value. In such a case it doubtless represents an accumulation of small indications, each so trifling or so evasive that the trader cannot clearly marshal and review them even in his own mind.

Only the experienced trader is entitled to a "hunch." The novice, or the man who is not closely in touch with technical conditions, is merely making an unusual ass of himself when he talks about a "hunch."

The successful trader gradually learns to study his own psychological characteristics and allow to some extent for his customary errors of judgment. If he finds that he is generally too hasty in reaching a conclusion, he learns to wait and reflect further. After making his decision, he withdraws it and lays it up on a shelf to ripen. He makes only a part of his full commitment at the moment when he feels most confident, holding the remainder in reserve.

If he finds that he is usually overcautious, he eventually learns to be a little more daring, to buy a part of his line while his mind is still partially enveloped in the mists of doubt.

Most of the practical suggestions which can be offered are necessarily of a somewhat negative character. We can point out the errors to be avoided much more successfully than we can lay out a course of positive action. But the following summary may be useful to the active trader:

(1) Your main purpose must be to keep the mind clear and well balanced. Hence, do not act hastily on apparently sensational information; do not trade so heavily as to become anxious; and do not permit yourself to be influenced by your position in the market.

(2) Act on your own judgment, or else act absolutely and entirely on the judgment of another, regardless of your own opinion. "Too many cooks spoil the broth."

(3) When in doubt, keep out of the market. Delays cost less than losses.

(4) Endeavor to catch the trend of sentiment. Even if this should be temporarily against fundamental condi-

tions, it is nevertheless unprofitable to oppose it.

(5) The greatest fault of ninety-nine out of one hundred active traders is being bullish at high prices and bearish at low prices. Therefore, refuse to follow the market beyond what you consider a reasonable climax, no matter how large the possible profits that you may appear to be losing by inaction.

The field covered by these chapters is to a great extent new. As it becomes more thoroughly cultivated, it may be possible to speak with more scientific definiteness. In the meantime, the author hopes that his comments and suggestions may be of some service in helping readers to avoid unwise risks and to apply sound principles of analysis to the investment or speculative situation.

Treasure of Books

Under One Roof

Demand
Any Rare Book
at

www.facsimilepublisher.com

Demand Any Rare Book at:

www.facsimilepublisher.com

if not available, give information,
our team will search and update you.

Promote Knowledge:

If you have any rare book
which is not available at
www.facsimilepublisher.com,
offer it to other readers so that others can also be
benefitted with your cooperation.
The book will be printed with your courtesy.

Print & Publish:

If you wish to get your book printed or published,
we have the service for you.

Customization on Demand:

We offer customization of books
as per the demand of the customer.

Published by

Facsimile Publisher
Ashok Vihar, Delhi-110052 (India)
Website: www.facsimilepublisher.com

Distributed by

Gyan Books Pvt. Ltd.
5, Ansari Road, Daryaganj, New Delhi-110002 (India)
E-mail: books@gyanbooks.com, Website: www.gyanbooks.com

4 444006 186232